What People Are Saying About

The Stupid Syndrome

The Stupid Syndrome is a clear, practical guide for leaders who want sharper decisions and real accountability. Gregory cuts through noise with frameworks that are immediately usable in complex environments. A timely, no-nonsense playbook.
Ben Grinnell, Head of Capabilities and AI at Newton

Straightforward frameworks that travel well—boardroom to frontline, public or private sector—so leaders can make sharper calls and own the outcomes.
Denise McDonagh, CBE, Former CIO, private and public sectors, and Non-executive Director

What People Are Saying About

The Stupid Syndrome

Why Smart Leaders Fall for the Wrong Ideas

The Stupid Syndrome

Why Smart Leaders Fall for the Wrong Ideas

by Gregory Henwood

Business Books
Winchester, UK
Washington, USA

CollectiveInk

First published by Business Books, 2026
Business Books is an imprint of Collective Ink Ltd.,
Unit 11, Shepperton House, 89 Shepperton Road, London, N1 3DF
office@collectiveink.com
www.collectiveink.com
www.collectiveink.com/business-books

For distributor details and how to order please visit the 'Ordering' section on our website.

ISBN: 978 1 80695 012 6
978 1 80695 013 3 (ebook)

A CIP catalogue record for this book is available from the British Library.

Design: Lapiz Digital Services

UK: Printed and bound by CPI Group (UK) Ltd, Croydon, CR0 4YY
Printed in North America by CPI GPS partners

The manufacturer's authorised representative in the EU for product safety is: eucomply OÜ - Pärnu mnt 139b-14, 11317 Tallinn, Estonia, hello@ eucompliancepartner.com, www.eucompliancepartner.com

We operate a distinctive and ethical publishing philosophy in all areas of our business, from our global network of authors to production and worldwide distribution.

This book is dedicated to:
My loving Family
TXOX

Thanks for the support

This book is entirely fictional. It's meant to capture common systemic failures in corporate decision-making. Rather than simply recounting events as they occurred, this book draws on the lessons I've learned throughout my career to explore how poor corporate decision-making is allowed to take root, and why it so often goes unchallenged. Any resemblance to real events is coincidental and unintentional.

Table of Contents

About the Author

H. Gregory Henwood is a distinguished technology and transformation leader with over two decades of experience driving innovation, operational excellence, and strategic growth across global industries. Based in Sussex, United Kingdom, Gregory has served in pivotal roles, including Group Chief Information and Operating Officer for multibillion-dollar organisations, where he has elevated IT from a cost centre to a core enabler of business success.

Recognised in the CIO UK 100 2025, Business & Finance CIO 100 Index 2024 & 2025 as one of Ireland's top digital leaders, Gregory has been at the forefront of ambitious digital transformations. He has a proven track record of streamlining operations, improving cybersecurity resilience, and spearheading large-scale projects, such as cloud migrations and organisational restructuring, that have delivered measurable results in cost savings, efficiency, and growth.

Gregory's career spans industries as diverse as financial services, manufacturing, and public sector transformation. His accolades include the Project and Programme Management Award and recognition for transformative contributions to criminal justice systems in the UK. Beyond the corporate world, Gregory has cultivated ventures like establishing a vineyard in New Zealand, showcasing his entrepreneurial spirit and diverse interests.

Driven by a passion for understanding human behaviour in business, Gregory's work explores the tension between truth and optimism in decision-making. This book builds on his extensive leadership experience to delve into why organisations and individuals often choose to believe convenient falsehoods over hard truths, offering unique insights into the psychology of business culture. Gregory's decades of experience have honed his ability to recognise and support the conditions that lead to sound corporate decision-making. The hard-earned insights he has gained throughout his career are thoughtfully embedded in this compelling fictional narrative.

About the Organisation for this Book

Kelvine Pharmaceuticals Group (KPG) is a global pharmaceutical company operating across more than 30 countries with combined revenues exceeding £14 billion. Headquartered in Rotterdam, KPG oversees two primary business units:

Kelvine Consumer Pharmaceuticals (KCP) - Responsible for retail-focused, high-volume pharmaceuticals and health products, supplying pharmacies and healthcare retailers.

Kelvine Institutional Pharmaceuticals (KIP) - The B2B arm, providing bulk pharmaceuticals and medical supplies to hospitals, healthcare institutions, and government contracts, operating under strict compliance and regulatory standards.

Both units share a centralised IT function under the group's corporate leadership. However, growing tensions between operational agility, compliance obligations, and the governance structure set the stage for internal challenges—and ultimately, a power struggle.

Note: Kelvine Pharmaceuticals Group (KPG), Kelvine Consumer Pharmaceuticals (KCP), and Kelvine Institutional Pharmaceuticals (KIP) are entirely fictional entities. Any resemblance to real companies, organisations, or individuals—living or dead—is purely coincidental.

Chapter One

I Am God

Stupid People

"Anyone who holds a true opinion without understanding is like a blind man on the right road."

Socrates

Introduction: A New Arrival

Marcus had been exhausted. This was his first overseas trip in his new role, a stage he had long prepared for. He knew that confidence alone wasn't enough—he needed to observe, adapt, and strike when the moment was right. The business was a puzzle, and he had every intention of solving it in his favour. The nervousness wasn't from fear of failure, but from impatience—he was eager to prove he belonged at the top. The organisation was abuzz with concerns about slow delivery and high costs of change. The North American executives had arrived in full force—COOs, CEOs, and leadership figures all eager to resolve their issues.

The previous feedback was blunt, funding was scarce, and the business lacked the ability to drive change. Marcus had heard the complaints before, but he saw them differently. Where others saw obstacles, he saw an opportunity to remove "dead weight." His talent was cutting through what he saw as unnecessary complexity. He had spent weeks studying their weaknesses. The IT team was slow, resistant, and too focused on policies rather than outcomes. If he could position himself as the "fixer," the leadership would turn to him instead. The IT team wasn't helping; they were delaying change. This was his chance to take control. Marcus, however, believed he had all the answers. He had skipped previous corporate meetings, deeming them unnecessary. He saw himself as more intelligent than most of his colleagues and viewed their input as tedious. He had little patience for people who, in his eyes, could not see the simple solutions he believed were obvious.

What Marcus hadn't shared was his compensation structure. A "transformation bonus" would vest on **contract signature**—not go-live—provided he landed a 10-year platform deal and booked "run-rate savings" by quarter-end. Delivery risk lived elsewhere. If the programme dragged, he could still leave with the ribbon cut and his bonus banked.

His tendency to dismiss people extended beyond the workplace. Even in his personal life, Marcus had little interest in those he did not deem useful. His wife's two children from a previous marriage irritated him. He had done everything to keep them at arm's length, ensuring they remained outside of his carefully constructed world. The less time he spent with them, the better. In fact, he had been instrumental in ensuring they were sent to live with their father full-time.

Marcus preferred efficiency. If something or someone was a roadblock, he would find a way to remove it.

The first half day was spent listening to the business areas across NA and their individual worries. They all sounded serious: Wi-Fi not working properly or laptops running slow or not being able to just get their support businesses third parties to just connect their laptops or dial into the network. This all seemed like valid requests and as he was now in charge, he agreed that he would just allow these to happen as his expertise would say, what harm would any of these changes have? The CTO Graham supported some of the future design and delivery challenges they needed to complete for the next year and, also, assisting with BARK TANA (a comprehensive enterprise software suite ERP that integrates core business processes – finance, supply chain, HR, sales etc.).

The Business Meeting Begins

The meeting had been called to address the growing frustrations of the business leadership. The first half of the day was spent listening to concerns from North America.

Alistair (CEO of Kelvine Consumer Pharmaceuticals (KCP): "Our teams are struggling. We have basic operational problems—Wi-Fi not working, laptops running slow, and third parties struggling to connect to our network. We need faster responses."

Marcus, in his usual blunt style, waved his hand dismissively: "That sounds like an easy fix. Why are we making such a big deal out of this? I'll approve all of these requests immediately. The harm in removing restrictions is minimal."

Graham (CTO), leaning forward: "Marcus, these aren't just technical issues. Some of these systems have been designed with security in mind. Removing restrictions could expose the company to unnecessary risks. Have we assessed the potential consequences?"

Marcus (rolling his eyes): "BARK TANA? I've attended BARK meetings and been to Gartner presentations. It's a simple system. The vendors provide all the guidance. Honestly, Graham, sometimes I think IT just enjoys making things more complicated than they need to be."

Graham, a veteran with 30 years of experience, stiffened at his condescending tone.

Graham: "You don't know what you're talking about, Marcus. You've been here for two weeks, and you're making assumptions without fully understanding the system. These are complex changes, especially with business data linking to finance. Some of these processes take months of development and testing."

Marcus's face darkened. He had never been challenged like this before.

Marcus (coldly): "I don't like your tone, Graham. I've done this before and know all about BARK. Every company's system is the same — there's no difference. Maybe you need to recheck your details and actually support what the business needs."

The room fell into silence. The business was clear to witness the disagreement between these strong characters with one from the business 30 years and running the IT department for 15 years, working in the factory and understanding and servicing the business for the last five. Then this new leader, who seemed to be strong in position yet the polar opposite in position to the person who was there for many years. The business, however, had been waiting a long time to get this unhooked as for many years they had been having to cut here cut there and IT kept coming back stating, "You need to invest in order to change." This, now with Marcus, seemed like it could be something that would align to their way of thinking. The CEO of NA mentioned, "I believe we should spend some more time together with the leadership team and discuss this opportunity further. How about we take this discussion to my office with the leadership, and we can make progress?"

A Shift in Leadership

The business executives, long frustrated by slow IT responses, viewed Marcus as a breath of fresh air.

Richard (CEO of Kelvine Institutional Pharmaceuticals (KIP): "I think we need more discussions between leadership and Marcus. Perhaps we take this conversation to my office and work out a more practical approach?"

Graham knew this was a calculated move. His experience and years of work had just been undermined in a matter of minutes.

Alistair: "Thank you, Graham, for your input. We'll get back to you once we align with Marcus on the best way forward."

Marcus smirked. He had just won his first battle. Graham would soon be removed from the picture.

Marcus: "This will be worth our time if we work together without IT slowing us down. Our metric is signed savings this quarter; delivery comes later. If we remove unnecessary approvals and security concerns, we can focus on what really matters—business delivery."

The leadership nodded in agreement.

Reorganizing the IT Function

That afternoon, Marcus sat with the business leaders, mapping out changes.

Testing and documentation would be reduced.

Third-party restrictions would be removed.

IT governance would be relaxed.

Meanwhile, the IT staff, who had dedicated years to building a secure and structured environment, were left out of the conversation.

Mark (Infrastructure Manager): "Does anyone know what's going on? We haven't been consulted on any of these changes."

In the IT office, the team watched the board's decision unfold.

Mark (Infrastructure Manager, muttering): "This isn't just a process change — this is a corporate coup."

Peter (CISO) exhaled. "And we're the ones who will be blamed when it fails."

Sarah (Enterprise Architect): "I just heard they're slashing the documentation process. That's going to create chaos."

James (Service Manager): "They're stripping governance, Mark. Marcus doesn't care about controls or security. He just wants to make an impression."

Marcus walked past the IT office, adjusting his tie in the reflection of a nearby screen.

Marcus (muttering to himself): "They'll be fine. They always complain about change."

Inside the IT office, frustration simmered. Many had dedicated years to ensuring systems were robust, compliant, and efficient. Dedication to systems that do not have the people who wrote them, or the company has long ceased. Now, their work was being discarded without consultation.

Sarah: "I just got an email. The weekly IT governance meetings are cancelled indefinitely."

Mark clenched his jaw.

Mark: "We need to push back. If we don't, this company is going to fall apart in six months."

Marcus had already moved on, heading for an early dinner with business executives who praised his ability to "cut through the red tape."

The IT team knew better.

Meeting with the CISO

A couple of days later, Marcus had a scheduled catch-up with Peter, the CISO. He wasn't particularly interested in security, but he had attended a Gartner conference where a CISO gave a basic presentation, and as far as he was concerned, that meant he understood the role.

He walked into the meeting, his mind already elsewhere, fixing his tie in the reflection of the glass wall before turning to Peter with a smile that didn't reach his eyes.

Marcus: "Hey Peter, how are you? You know, I've never really understood what you do, but I'm sure you've got it under control. How many staff do you have?"

Peter, who had spent years meticulously building a capable security team, frowned slightly.

Peter: "Hi Marcus, I'm well. We have 65 people globally, managing cybersecurity, compliance, risk assessments, and security architecture."

Marcus let out a small laugh, shaking his head.

Marcus: "65? That seems excessive. What do they actually do? I mean, security is mostly just policies and monitoring, right?"

Peter exhaled sharply, sensing where this conversation was going.

Peter: "We handle global security threats daily, ensuring compliance across all regions and mitigating risks from both external and internal threats. Cyber threats are evolving, and our structure ensures we remain ahead of them."

Marcus barely listened. He was already calculating how he could pitch a reduction in headcount to the business.

Marcus (casually): "Well, I think we might be able to streamline that. Maybe consolidate the team down to 10 or so people? And possibly outsource parts of it? I have people who I am sure will be able to do a better job and cheaper from India."

Peter's expression hardened.

Peter: "Marcus, reducing security coverage that drastically would expose the whole company to significant risk. Security isn't just about firewalls and monitoring—it's about proactive threat management, compliance adherence, and protecting sensitive data."

Marcus (shrugging): "Look, I don't want to step into your world, so I'll let you handle it. But I had a meeting with North America's leadership, and they want to remove restrictions on third-party access. They believe security controls are slowing them down. We need to allow external vendors easier access to our systems."

Peter sat back, his eyes narrowing.

Peter: "That's the first I've heard of it. Removing those restrictions could open us up to potential attacks. Were security risks even considered?"

Marcus: "Of course. The business is comfortable with the risk. It's not that bad. The sentiment on the ground is that maybe we should even roll back some of the controls put in place after the last attack. Things have moved on."

Peter's stomach sank. This was reckless.

Peter: "I'll need to speak to leadership directly before we make such a change. Security risks aren't just an inconvenience; they can have catastrophic consequences."

Marcus (smiling but firm): "I'll handle leadership. Just get ready for the change. The decision has already been made."

As he walked out, Peter sat in silence, already knowing this would be a battle he would likely lose. The headcount cuts were not just a philosophy; they were a commitment he'd already trailed to finance. Hitting that number unlocked the first tranche of his bonus even if controls were rebuilt later under "phase two".

Scene: Incident Africa – Expanding Control

A Growing Influence

Three weeks had passed since Marcus's successful trip to the USA. The business had given glowing reviews of his performance to the executive committee, reinforcing his belief that taking over the IT function entirely was only a matter of time. By positioning himself as the one who could "get things done," he was quickly making changes that, in his mind, gave the business what it truly needed—without the constraints of process, governance, or oversight.

One of the key parts of his plan was a meeting he had already arranged with an external service provider, offering IT support on a demand basis. The goal? To cut costs by replacing in-house functions with a cheaper alternative, a move he saw as an obvious efficiency. He didn't believe in rigid contracts or structured agreements; in his opinion, they only slowed things down. As long as the business was happy, he looked good.

Africa was the next step in his strategy. The region had seen heavy investment over the last two years, and while some applications sat within the core business infrastructure, many others operated as independent projects. To Marcus, this was an opportunity to take full control.

Meeting with the African Leadership Team

The executive meeting in Africa was called to discuss how IT should support the business moving forward. As Marcus entered the room, he glanced around at the gathered executives. Among them was Solomon, a senior leader in the region, along with a mix of local CEOs, COOs, and finance representatives.

Solomon (CEO of Africa Operations): "We need to simplify things, Marcus. The group-wide controls and security restrictions don't help us—they help corporate, not Africa. We need autonomy to manage IT the way it suits our operations."

Marcus (nodding): "I completely agree. The bureaucracy around IT approvals has only slowed down progress. What do you propose?"

Solomon: "We need to recreate a small, dedicated team here—what we used to call 'special forces'—who can move fast, make system changes as needed, and bypass the layers of corporate approvals."

Marcus (smiling): "That makes perfect sense. I see no reason why we should be bound by unnecessary constraints. If you're comfortable removing some of these processes, then so am I. Less oversight means less delay."

Solomon leaned back in his chair, pleased. The discussion was heading in exactly the direction he wanted.

Solomon: "We also need to reinstate some of our previous suppliers. Certain contracts were removed under corporate cost-saving measures, and frankly, it's hurt our ability to operate smoothly."

Marcus nodded again.

Marcus: "I understand. The supplier decisions should be made locally, not dictated from corporate. If these vendors help the business move faster, I'll support bringing them back."

One of the finance representatives cleared his throat.

Finance Lead: "Marcus, won't corporate push back on these decisions? Some of these security controls and cost restrictions were implemented at the highest levels."

Marcus (waving his hand dismissively): "I've already spoken to leadership in North America. If they're comfortable with the risk, then it's not an issue. The noise I've been hearing suggests we may even be able to scale back some of the compliance controls put in place after the last cyberattack. Things have moved on since then."

A few heads turned at that comment. Peter, the CISO, had made it clear that certain security controls were non-negotiable, and yet here was Marcus, effectively deciding to ignore them.

The European Connection

Later that afternoon, Marcus had a private call with Albert Reynolds, the European CEO. He knew he had long been frustrated with IT's slow pace and saw an opportunity to align their interests.

Albert Reynolds: "Marcus, I've been speaking with BARK, and they assure me the move to TANA isn't as expensive as IT keeps saying. They're offering us a migration plan for only £15 million all-inclusive as long as we sign for 10 years. Why are we even considering the £100 million approach?"

Marcus: "I completely agree, Albert. The IT team loves to overcomplicate things. I've migrated an entire company to TANA in four months for only £15 million. No lawyers, no expensive consultants—just action."

Albert: "Exactly! I knew I could count on you to cut through the nonsense. Let's move forward with the BARK deal and get it done quickly. I'll handle any internal pushback."

Marcus smirked to himself. This was working perfectly.

Undermining the IT Function

Back at corporate headquarters, the IT team had begun to notice changes rolling through the organisation—changes they had no say in.

Mark (Infrastructure Manager): "Did anyone hear about the security policy rollback? I just saw an update that third-party access restrictions are being removed."

Sarah (Enterprise Architect): "Nope. We weren't consulted. I just got an email cancelling the next security compliance review."

James (Service Manager): "This is madness. The governance board hasn't even met to approve any of this. Who authorized it?"

Mark: "Marcus."

Silence. Then, finally, Sarah sighed.

Sarah: "This is going to end badly."

Scene: The TANA Meeting – Pushing the Deal

Gathering the Executives

The executives from across the regions—Europe, North America, Africa, and South America—had gathered for a high-level discussion on BARK TANA. The meeting included the CEOs of KIP and KCP, the Group CFO (GCFO), and Marcus's key ally in Europe. This wasn't a scheduled review; Marcus had orchestrated the discussion outside of normal governance structures, ensuring that decision-makers were in the room without the current CIO's involvement.

He adjusted his blazer, smoothed his tie, and took a breath before beginning. He needed this to go his way.

Marcus's Proposal

Marcus: "Thank you all for joining on such short notice. I know this isn't our usual process, but I wanted to bring us together to discuss a unique opportunity. There have been various discussions around the cost of BARK TANA, and I know there's concern over the high estimates we've received. However, after working closely with our European leadership, I can confidently say that those numbers are inflated."

He glanced around, ensuring he had their attention before continuing.

Marcus: "The current CIO and the NY consultancy have provided estimates that put the migration at upwards of £150 million, but based on my experience, I can tell you that this is completely unnecessary. I have personally led a successful migration in my last company, and it didn't take nearly as much effort or money as they are suggesting. With the right approach, we can complete this project in just three months, at a total cost of £15 million."

He clicked a button on his laptop, bringing up a slide with simplified figures.

"We've already engaged TCR (a large multinational service delivery company), who have agreed to deliver the entire migration for £10 million. Our internal team will handle another portion for £2 million, and BARK has already agreed to support the additional system licensing at £3 million. This is a no-brainer—it's a fraction of what we were originally told, and it's fast."

Marcus: "Based on prior calls, BARK will extend a 45% end-of-quarter discount if we sign by Friday. TCR has pre-allocated a delivery squad through quarter-close—miss the window and rates revert."

Group CFO: "Discounts tied to signature before quarter-close usually mean testing, change and hypercare aren't in scope. Show me the SOW line-items for data cleansing, business change, testing and hypercare—or this isn't comparable."

He could see some nods around the table, but not everyone was convinced.

Pushback from Leadership

Group CFO (leaning forward): "Marcus, this completely contradicts what we've been told by both the CIO and the consultancy firms we've engaged. Why would we suddenly change course when the current strategy is based on detailed analysis and industry benchmarks?"

Marcus (smiling, but firm): "I understand your hesitation, but let's be honest things have changed. The suppliers and TCR are ready to move forward immediately. They have assured us that this can be done within the timeframe and the budget we've outlined. Their incentives align with ours—they want this deal closed before the end of the year, and it benefits us to act quickly."

He turned to the CEO of KIP, whose expression remained sceptical.

CEO of KIP: "I'll stay out of this since it primarily impacts KCP, but I have to say—this sounds too good to be true. A deal that moves this quickly and has this many decision-makers forced into a single room always reminds me of something that will go horribly wrong."

Marcus exhaled quietly. He needed to move past him and secure the others.

CEO of KCP (considering): "I'm no technical expert, but this whole conversation about £150 million plus to move to TANA always seemed excessive. Marcus, from what we've discussed previously, you seem to have a much better understanding of the actual costs. If you're saying this can be done at a fraction of the cost, I'm happy to move forward."

Marcus smiled internally. This was exactly what he needed.

CEO of KCP: "We should advise the CIO of our decision, but frankly, I nominate Rob to take this forward since he has been working closely with the CIO and IT leadership. Rob, can you handle that?"

Rob (Operations Director, nodding): "Of course. But if we're doing this, I suggest that, Prita and I initiate the wider plan we discussed for additional cost-saving measures alongside this migration."

As Marcus listened to the executives voice their concerns, he mentally mapped out the power dynamics in the room. Who was sceptical? Who was passive? Who could be swayed? This wasn't just a meeting—it was an opportunity.

Marcus leaned back, satisfied. The deal was moving forward. The CIO wouldn't find out until it was too late to stop it. The next phase of his plan was beginning to take shape.

Scene: The Family – A Carefully Controlled World

Marcus had never been one for family. When he met Julia, he saw her as a woman of means, a pathway to a life of luxury. But her two children were an unexpected and unwelcome addition to the perfect world he'd envisioned. To him, they were disruptive elements, blemishes on an otherwise carefully curated existence.

From the beginning, he made it clear—this was his life, and they were merely visitors. The first few years were tolerable; he performed the role of the charming stepfather when necessary, ensuring Julia saw what he wanted to see. But inside, resentment simmered. The charade of familial warmth exhausted him.

Their marriage was fast-tracked. Within two months of dating, Julia had proposed and he had been swept up in the thrill of a woman who knew exactly how to make him feel like the centre of her universe. The wedding was in Vegas, an impulsive move on his part, pitched as a spontaneous, romantic adventure but, in truth, a strategic manoeuvre. He had secured his position.

When the news reached her children, the reaction was immediate and hostile. They didn't speak to their mother for months, furious that they had been left out of such a significant decision. Marcus dismissed their anger as childish entitlement.

Marcus (mocking): "They didn't pay for the wedding, so why should they get a say?"

It took a year of expensive gifts and appeasements for Julia to mend things with them. But Marcus remained indifferent. Their presence was tolerated, but only because it was unavoidable.

Redefining the Home:

The grand estate was now his domain. He ensured that when the children visited, they were kept at a distance—both physically and emotionally. He had insisted that they stay in the guest house, away from the main property. Julia initially protested, but he framed it as a practical decision, "giving them their own space," while it was about keeping his world undisturbed.

He had worked hard to integrate himself into Julia's financial affairs. The Trust company had been a particularly strategic move. If anything were to happen, he had voting rights on the beneficiaries, something he had orchestrated with precision. He had played the long game, and it had paid off.

The children were oblivious to this. He saw no need to tell them. Why complicate things?

Marcus (to himself): "It's not as if they'd understand finance anyway."

His approach to them was transactional—keep them appeased just enough so they didn't interfere. He bought them expensive gifts on occasion, a habit he had learned from Julia. It was easier that way; sentiment required effort, money did not.

A Carefully Maintained Illusion:

Julia remained blissfully unaware of Marcus's true feelings. He saw what he wanted to see—an elegant, refined woman who had brought excitement into his life. He played the role expertly.

His marriage wasn't built on love; it was built on control. From the way he presented himself to the way he managed their social circles, everything was calculated. He spent more time curating his wardrobe and attending networking events than he ever did thinking about family dynamics.

On the rare occasions that Julia's children were around, he tolerated their presence with the detached patience of someone enduring an inconvenience.

Marcus (internally sighing as they arrived): "A weekend of forced pleasantries. How lovely."

But it wasn't a long-term concern. They were growing older, their visits becoming less frequent. Soon, they would be nothing more than distant figures in Julia's life.

And that was exactly how Marcus wanted it.

Scene: HR Discussion – Reshaping the Structure

A Strategic Conversation

The HR Lead for the company, Shina leaned back in their chair, studying Marcus with a measured look.

Shina: "Marcus, it's been two weeks since you joined, and I've been hearing some great feedback from the senior teams in both the U.S. and Europe. They're impressed with how you're challenging the status quo. How are you settling in?"

Marcus smiled, knowing this was the opening he needed.

Marcus: "It's been interesting, lots of discussions, and I'm really enjoying it. I see so many opportunities to refine how we operate. I've been listening, and I genuinely think there's an opportunity to improve the model for staff. The way things are structured now just doesn't work."

Shina raised an eyebrow.

Shina: "That's a bold statement. We've spent a significant amount of time designing this model to drive efficiency and financial alignment. What specifically do you think isn't working?"

Marcus exhaled dramatically, leaning forward.

Marcus: "We've invested in a model designed to create savings, but it's only half-built. There are still 60 open roles that haven't been filled. Maybe that's why it's not delivering. But the real issue? The people in key positions don't have the technical capability to take us forward."

Shina frowned slightly, sensing where this was going.

Shina: "Are you saying the leadership team isn't up to the task?"

Marcus's tone was firm.

Marcus: "That's exactly what I'm saying. Look at what we have—an outdated infrastructure team led by someone stuck in the 80s, a CTO who doesn't understand technology at scale, an applications lead who has no real BARK experience, and a service lead who spends more time talking about how great he is than actually delivering. And let's not even start on the CISO—someone who isn't technical and has no real grasp on modern security threats."

Shina's fingers tapped the desk lightly.

Shina: "That's quite an assessment. And what's your proposed solution?"

Marcus sat back, crossing his legs as if this were the simplest decision in the world.

Marcus: "We strip the headcount and create a different model. I would take direct responsibility for KCP, and someone else can handle KIP. There's no reason for a central structure—

it just slows things down. I've already discussed this with Rob, and he's supportive. He's agreed to take over operations, network, and service management. Everyone wins."

Shina hesitated. The idea of such a dramatic shift was concerning, but they had to admit Marcus had a knack for cutting through the noise.

Shina: "That would be a major change. I know the senior executives have been frustrated. The GCIO has been a roadblock in their eyes, always pushing back on cost-saving measures. The IT team is meeting their quotas, but the leadership feels restricted. They want more freedom to make decisions and changes to whatever they like in the estate."

Marcus smirked.

Marcus: "Exactly. The GCIO keeps saying no. No to savings, no to flexibility, no to the business getting what it wants. But let's be honest—the business doesn't care about IT structures; they care about manufacturing and distributing pharmaceuticals and healthcare products, about delivering compliance and quality products. IT should be there to support, not control."

Shina nodded slowly.

Shina: "There's a lot to consider here. Changing the structure would mean rewriting the operating model entirely."

Marcus leaned in.

Marcus: "Let's take this to leadership and see what they say. We have a chance to make a fundamental shift here. Since I've arrived, I think you've seen the impact I can make. We should capitalize on that momentum."

Shina sighed, considering the implications.

Shina: "Alright. Let's explore it. But you know this won't be easy. The IT function will push back. The GCIO will push back."

Marcus smiled again, knowing he had already won half the battle.

Marcus: "They always do. But in the end, they won't have a choice."

Scene: Restructuring the IT Model

A Leadership Meeting with Big Decisions

The executives gathered in the boardroom, the air thick with anticipation. There had been whispers of change for weeks, but today was the day decisions would be made. The leadership team was present—CEOs from KIP and KCP, the Group CFO, and Marcus, who had been steadily positioning himself at the centre of the discussion.

Meeting Host: "Thank you all for joining today. I know everyone is busy, so I'll get straight to it. Over the past month, I've had discussions with Marcus regarding a shift in our IT model. Though he's new to the organisation, we've all seen how he works—efficiently, effectively, and most importantly, with cost reductions in mind. He's done this before, and it's time we take a fresh approach. We're not saying the GCIO isn't capable, but times have changed, and our structure may need to evolve to better support the business. Marcus, over to you."

Marcus nodded, a self-assured smile crossing his face as he stood and addressed the room.

Marcus: "Thank you all for your time. I won't waste it—let's cut to the chase. The IT structure, as it stands today, is not working. The centralized global model is outdated, bureaucratic, and unresponsive to the needs of the business. Across the group, I've heard the same complaints—IT is slow, rigid, and constantly pushing back on business-driven change. The GCIO and his team create unnecessary obstacles with process and budget constraints, limiting our ability to move at the speed the business requires."

He paused, letting his words settle before continuing.

Marcus: "Each business should have the freedom to operate IT the way they need to. If we want people to install software, they should be able to do it without red tape. If we need infrastructure changes, they shouldn't require a committee's approval. The reality is the business teams know what they need better than IT does. This industry myth that IT should steer business decisions. It's outdated and ineffective."

He let that statement linger before moving to his next point.

Marcus: "I'm proposing a complete restructuring of IT. We remove two key leadership positions—the Applications Lead and the Group CIO—and devolve their responsibilities. I will oversee KCP operations directly, while another leader can take responsibility for KIP. This removes unnecessary complexity and allows each business to take control of its own IT needs."

There were murmurs across the table as some leaned in, intrigued, while others exchanged sceptical glances.

Marcus (continuing): "I've spoken with TCR, and they've offered a combined deal. If we commit to the BARK migration programme with them, they'll deliver a full restructuring of the IT model at no extra charge. That includes removing the Group CIO and Applications Director roles—an immediate £1.5 million cost saving. This isn't just tactical; it's structural. It simplifies the hierarchy, removes bottlenecks, and puts delivery closer to where the business actually operates."

He sat back, confident in the numbers he had put forward. Now it was time for the response.

As emails congratulated the "quick win," Marcus drafted a polite reply to a recruiter; his retention milestone would be met long before cutover.

Dissent and Agreement

CEO of KIP (folding his arms): "Well, from my team's perspective, we've struggled to get IT to align with what we need for the past year. We keep hitting the same walls—budget restrictions, process delays, and approvals that take months. So, Marcus, I can see why this approach makes sense. You have my support, and I expect the leadership team will agree."

CEO of KCP (nodding in agreement): "I'm in the same boat. The room had heard the same complaints for months—delays, bureaucracy, inefficiencies. But today was different. Marcus had managed to frame it as more than just an inconvenience—it was an existential threat to business growth. The question was no longer whether IT should change, but how fast to push change. We can't afford that kind of resistance anymore. Marcus, your plan is bold, but I think it's exactly what we need. You have my support as well."

Group CFO (raising a hand): "I do have concerns. We put the current model in place to reduce costs and streamline IT functions. I'm not saying the GCIO, and his team have done everything perfectly, but this approach is a drastic change. We've been meeting our financial targets, and this shift could create new risks. Are we sure this model won't lead to uncontrolled spending or security gaps?"

CEO of KIP (leaning forward): "Look, we can't keep managing operations through budget cuts alone. At some point, we have to acknowledge that the rigidity of IT is costing us more than it's saving."

Zeb (Senior Operations Lead, speaking up for the first time): "We tried the centralized model, and it worked for a while. But now, we need something more agile, something that truly supports how our businesses operate. The TCR-backed model is a logical step forward."

Group CFO (after a pause): "Alright, then. It sounds like the agreement is to move forward with this model."

A final round of nods followed. The decision had been made.

Chapter Two

The Tablets

Undeniable

Scene: Executive Review Meeting

The senior IT and business leaders gathered in the executive boardroom for a critical presentation. The meeting was orchestrated by the IT group on behalf of the business, bringing together key figures: the infrastructure specialist, the service delivery manager, the change lead, the group CIO, the applications lead, and the commercial lead for IT. Across from them sat the CEOs and COOs of the two businesses, waiting to hear the findings of a four-month analysis conducted by TY, a consultancy firm specializing in BARK migrations. They had been working on the task for four months prior to Marcus's arrival. The atmosphere was tense, with some leaders sceptical of the projected costs and effort, while others remained eager to validate the findings and proceed cautiously.

Opening the Meeting

Group CIO: "Thank you all for joining. Over the past four months, TY has conducted a thorough assessment of the BARK TANA migration plan, reviewing system licences, infrastructure topology, and associated costs. This initiative was led by the IT group to ensure alignment with business needs. Today, we will present TY's findings, outline a proposed approach, and take your questions. Let's get started."

Change Lead: "We structured the review around three core elements: the best approach for migration based on our current estate, the time and cost required for implementation, and the work required to get the organisation's requirements ready for transition."

Infrastructure Specialist: "TY deployed industry-standard analysis tools to extract data across all EC2 instances. Their team, which has performed similar migrations for companies of comparable size, validated this data against real-world examples. The evidence shows that a properly executed migration is expected to exceed £100 million in total investment."

Service Delivery Manager: "These costs reflect not just licensing but also the necessary transformations in business processes, system testing, and risk mitigation. Cutting corners would likely result in extended delays, unforeseen costs, and operational risks."

Presenting the Findings

The infrastructure specialist displayed a detailed breakdown on the large screen.

Applications Lead: "Our analysis aligns closely with industry trends. TY observed similar BARK TANA migration projects at large enterprises, including a £320 million project at a global pharmaceutical manufacturing firm and a £390 million transformation at a leading international pharmaceutical company. Business readiness and process alignment account for the bulk of these costs."

Commercial Lead: "While the costs are significant, this investment must be evaluated against the risks of staying with the current infrastructure. Extended BARK support costs will rise exponentially post-2027, and operational inefficiencies will continue to drain resources."

Group CIO: "The question we must ask ourselves is not just about cost—but about long-term business agility. If we delay, we will fall behind our competitors who are already leveraging TANA's capabilities."

A Challenge from Leadership

Albert Reynolds (European CEO) leaned forward, sceptical: "We've received multiple cost estimates from industry studies and analysts, and this one is dramatically lower. BARK claims this can be done cost-effectively, but TY and Gartner analysis suggest otherwise. If I sign off on this, I need more than one perspective—what's driving these discrepancies?"

Change Lead: "BARK's approach oversimplifies the process. Buying the license is just the beginning. Our infrastructure requires customization, extensive data migration, and system testing to ensure business continuity."

Alistair (CEO of KCP): "But I've heard that similar companies have moved to the cloud without such high costs. We've spoken to firms who claim they did this with minimal teams and significantly less expenditure."

Infrastructure Specialist: "We reviewed companies that attempted to cut costs by skipping business process transformation. The result? They faced multi-year delays, and their total cost exceeded original estimates. Our plan avoids those pitfalls."

Service Delivery Manager: "We've seen what happens when organisations rush into cloud migrations assuming a simple 'lift and shift' approach. Companies that underestimated business process realignment found themselves stuck, unable to go live without massive emergency costs to fix unaccounted-for issues."

The Cost of Rushing the Process

Richard (CEO of KIP): "What happens if we push forward on a minimal budget and attempt a 'lift and shift' approach?"

Service Delivery Manager: "The risk is operational failure. Companies that underestimated business process realignment found themselves stuck, unable to go live without massive emergency costs to fix unaccounted-for issues. We've seen cost overruns of 200% in such cases."

Albert Reynolds: "I moved an organisation to EC2 twelve years ago, and we did it for far less. Why should this be any different?"

Group CIO: "Albert, moving to EC2 is different from transforming enterprise business processes onto TANA. Your previous move was an infrastructure migration, not a full BARK redesign. We must account for finance, procurement, logistics, and compliance."

Prita Patel (GCFO), cleared her throat: "If this goes wrong, it won't just be a licensing issue—it'll impact our ability to process transactions, manage finances, and integrate with supply chains. Have we run a full operational risk assessment, or are we just assuming this will work?"

Case Study 1: PharmaCare Group (Pharmaceutical Manufacturing)

- ✓ Revenue: £10 billion
- ✓ Migration Cost: £320 million, including £150 million in business process realignment.
- ✓ Challenges: Misaligned processes led to multiple delays, requiring expensive reengineering.
- ✓ Lesson: Investing in transformation upfront saves money in the long run.

Case Study 2: Global Pharma Corporation

- ✓ Migration Cost: £390 million, with £180 million allocated to business process change.
- ✓ Success Factor: Engaging stakeholders early and implementing a phased rollout prevented major disruptions.

✓ Lesson: Comprehensive stakeholder engagement and phased delivery reduce risks.

Closing Discussion and Next Steps

Prita Patel (GCFO): "Again, we need to ensure that any decision we take is backed by both financial prudence and operational sustainability. While we want cost savings, the risks associated with a rushed migration could end up costing us more."

Service Delivery Manager: "Our next step should be to refine the business case based on today's discussion. We need clear alignment on approach and risk appetite before proceeding further."

Group CIO: "Agreed. Let's document the concerns raised today, refine the cost breakdown, and bring a revised plan to the board next week."

Albert Reynolds: "Fine, but I still want BARK's viewpoint included. We should compare what they claim against what you're presenting."

Group CIO: "Of course. We'll validate with multiple sources before finalizing our approach."

As the meeting concluded, the leadership team acknowledged the challenges ahead. While some remained sceptical, the evidence presented pointed toward a structured and cautious approach rather than a rushed, cost-cutting decision. The next stage would be crucial in determining how the organisation would proceed with BARK TANA migration.

Prita Patel wasn't convinced. During a private follow-up, she raised concerns with the KCP CEO.

Prita: "If this fails, we'll be explaining a hundred-million-pound loss to the board. We need more than Marcus's word on this."

Chapter Three

The Protagonist's Belief

Scene: Leadership Team Meeting

Is Reality, Reality?

The IT leadership team gathered for Marcus's presentation on the BARK TANA migration plan for his previous company. The room included key figures: the infrastructure specialist, the service delivery manager, the change lead, the group CIO, the applications lead, and the commercial lead for IT. Tension was palpable, as Marcus's peers were eager to understand the project's scope and his ability to lead such a critical initiative. Some, however, carried scepticism about his claims.

Before the presentation began, an anonymous email circulated among the leadership team—a detailed document questioning the validity of Marcus's claims. It listed past failed migrations, miscalculated cost savings, and unsupported claims of success. As the meeting started, some leaders began to question whether Marcus's plan was a strategic move or a reckless gamble.

The Presentation Begins

Marcus began confidently, presenting a slide deck that outlined the migration's advantages and a timeline for delivery. He emphasized his past experiences and assured the team that his approach was well-founded.

Infrastructure Specialist: "Marcus, your slide compares this migration to a company operating at high trade volumes, but we're dealing with a completely different infrastructure. How does this align with our low-volume, high-cost model?"

Marcus (brushing it off): "That's irrelevant. We deal with more trades than you're considering. Let's move on."

He clicked to the next slide, which showcased an aggressive timeline: migration starting in February and completing by November 2024.

Service Delivery Manager: "Marcus, didn't you leave your previous organisation at the end of 2023? How could you have overseen a project that extends into 2024?"

Marcus (with irritation): "I handled the contracting phase. That gives me full insight into how these projects work."

Change Lead: "So, to clarify, you managed the agreements but not the actual implementation? That's an important distinction."

Marcus (defensively): "Let's not get caught up in semantics. I know how these migrations function."

A murmur spread across the room as the leadership team exchanged glances. The Procurement Lead turned to the Infrastructure Specialist and whispered, "Are we seriously considering this approach here? He hasn't presented a single real-world benchmark." The Service Delivery Manager sighed, "We should press for more details. If we don't, this becomes our problem when it falls apart."

Probing Questions

As the presentation continued, the cracks in Marcus's narrative became more apparent. His peers began to question his plans in greater detail.

Applications Lead: "Marcus, you mentioned streamlining data migration. Can you elaborate on how you plan to manage legacy system compatibility? We've had significant issues with that in past projects."

Marcus: "It's all outlined in the presentation.

Applications Lead: "The slides were vague on specifics. Could you walk us through the technical details?"

Marcus (snapping): "If you had paid attention, you'd already understand. I don't have time to explain every little detail."

Group CIO: "Marcus, this potential future project is a top priority. Addressing the technical details from your past will help us anticipate challenges later."

Marcus (dismissing): "We have bigger things to focus on. Let's not waste time nitpicking."

Financial Concerns

Commercial Lead: "Marcus, can you break down the £15 million cost estimate? Transparency will help us align budgets."

Marcus: "The figures are accurate. Everything has been accounted for."

Commercial Lead: "But can we see the itemized breakdown? It's important for resource allocation."

Marcus (visibly annoyed): "I don't have the breakdown with me right now. Trust my word—it's all accurate."

The Commercial Lead cleared his throat: "We're discussing millions in cost reductions, but we have yet to see a detailed breakdown of expenses. If these projections are wrong, we could face budget overruns that wipe out any perceived savings. Can we afford that risk?"

Marcus gave a tight-lipped smile. "We've accounted for everything. Let's not get caught up in unnecessary concerns. It's time to act."

Group CIO: "Trust is important, but we need concrete numbers to support this scale of investment. Can you provide a detailed cost breakdown by end of day?"

Marcus (glowering): "I'll try, but no promises."

Escalating Tensions

As the meeting progressed, frustration among the team grew. Marcus's dismissive tone and lack of detailed responses only deepened their concerns.

Service Delivery Manager: "Marcus, how did you plan to ensure seamless integration with our existing service workflows?"

Marcus: "That's already covered."

Service Delivery Manager: "I don't see a concrete plan for that delivery in the slides. Integration is critical to avoiding downtime."

Marcus (snapping): "You're overcomplicating things."

The atmosphere in the room grew tense. His peers exchanged uneasy glances, realizing that critical gaps in planning were being ignored.

Before the meeting concluded, Peter (CISO) leaned forward: "We can't just approve this without a contingency plan. The risks extend beyond cost—we're looking at system security vulnerabilities, operational downtime, and long-term compliance failures.' The Infrastructure Specialist nodded. 'Even if we move forward, we need mitigation strategies in place before rollout."

But before anyone could respond, Marcus tapped his pen against the table. 'The decision has been made already with the seniors. We're moving forward. Let's not waste any more time.'"

All the meeting attendees paid immediate attention.

Group CIO: "Can we chat later about this, Marcus? I want to understand this comment."

Post-Meeting Discussions

After the meeting, the team gathered to debrief. Their collective frustration was evident.

Infrastructure Specialist: "He's avoiding accountability. I'm not convinced he was involved and can support the details presented from the previous delivery."

Group CIO: "We need to document our concerns thoroughly. I'll escalate this to the executive level. Transparency is non-negotiable."

Change Lead: "Let's ensure we highlight specific gaps—like the lack of detailed cost breakdowns and integration strategies."

The team nodded in agreement. Determined to protect the organisation's interests, they resolved to push for clarity and accountability if such a decision has been made. The stakes were too high to allow Marcus's evasive approach to derail the industry standards they had been following and the future projects.

Closing Thought

The meeting had revealed more questions than answers. Marcus's dismissive attitude and unwillingness to address critical concerns left the team unsettled. As they prepared to escalate their issues, one thing was clear: ensuring the success of the BARK TANA migration would require vigilance, collaboration, and a commitment to transparency. Marcus had won this battle with the EXCO, but he knew the real challenge lay ahead continuing with convincing the global leadership team that his vision was the only path forward.

Chapter Four

The Industry's Predicament

Scene: A Boardroom in a High-Rise Office

What Facts, Gartner's?

The room is filled with senior COOs and CXOs representing major industries, gathered to hear Gartner analysts present on the looming BARK TANA migration deadline. The atmosphere is tense, as leaders are eager to uncover actionable insights with the 2027 deadline fast approaching. The stakes are high, with significant financial implications tied to the migration—or lack thereof. Laptops hum softly, the faint glow of PowerPoint slides reflecting on the polished table.

Introduction by Gartner Analysts

Gartner Analyst 1: "Ladies and gentlemen, thank you for joining us. The BARK TANA migration deadline is rapidly approaching. Failure to meet the 2027 timeline will result in pharmaceutical organisations facing... higher costs related to extended support, regulatory non-compliance, and delays in product approvals—at substantially higher costs. BARK's incentives for transitioning customers, combined with increasing pressure from industry peers, make this an urgent matter."

Gartner Analyst 2: "Let's be clear. BARK employees are driven by bonuses tied directly to the creation of new TANA customers—whether through migration or greenfield implementations. This financial motivation intensifies the urgency but often leads to unrealistic expectations."

Table 1. **Common Vendor Incentives & How to Counter**		
What you'll hear (pitch)	**What it really means**	**How to counter (use all three)**
"EOQ discount ends Friday."	Quota pressure; compressed decision cycle; avoids scrutiny.	1) 60–90-day price hold; 2) decide after independent estimate; 3) no-penalty slip if scope expands.
"All-in migration for £X."	Licence + thin PS; change/testing out of scope.	1) Scope matrix (data, change, testing, hypercare); 2) WBS with named deliverables; 3) holdbacks tied to outcomes.
"Pre-allocated squad ready now."	Resource reuse; push to sign now; quality not guaranteed.	1) Name & lock key people; 2) Approve substitutes; 3) Service credits for churn.
"We did this at £Y elsewhere."	Different context/ scope; cherry-picked case.	1) Apples-to-apples scope compare; 2) Call the delivery lead; 3) Share risk log.
"Go-live in 3–6 months."	Assumes no process redesign; testing collapsed.	1) Non-functional test plan; 2) Cutover rehearsal; 3) Hypercare gate with budget.
"Risk on us — fixed price."	Margin recouped via change orders.	1) Change-order caps; 2) Explicit inclusions/ exclusions; 3) Earned-value reporting.

Dialogue: The Cost of Migration

Prita Patel (GCFO): "When we hear numbers like £100 million or more for migrations, how can mid-sized firms like ours compete? Is there a way to control these costs?"

Gartner Analyst 1: "The cost challenge is universal, Prita. Many companies make the critical mistake of replicating old-world processes into the new platform. This results in high migration expenses without delivering the efficiencies or returns promised. Real savings come from rethinking processes, not just moving them."

Alistair (CEO of KCP): "What about supplier costs? We've heard horror stories of costs doubling due to unexpected issues. How do we prevent that?"

Gartner Analyst 2: "Alistair, you're right to be concerned. Supplier contracts need to include detailed contingencies for adaptation issues. Robust vendor management and clear accountability frameworks are crucial. Most cost overruns occur because organisations fail to anticipate integration complexities."

Albert Reynolds (European CEO): "If we can define our processes clearly upfront, will that eliminate the risks entirely? Or do you think there's always a hidden 'gotcha' in the fine print?"

Gartner Analyst 1 (chuckling): "There's always a 'gotcha,' Albert. As one CIO once said, 'The devil isn't in the details; the devil is in the missing details.' Even the best-prepared plans will encounter unforeseen challenges, especially in areas like legacy system compatibility."

Dialogue: Balancing the Present and Future

Richard (CEO of KIP): "If the costs and complexities are so daunting, why even consider TANA? Why not stick with extended support until necessary?"

Gartner Analyst 1: "Richard, extended support is a temporary solution. Beyond the cost, delaying the migration risks losing competitive advantages. TANA's capabilities—from real-time analytics to streamlined workflows—position organisations to respond faster to market demands. The long-term benefits outweigh the short-term savings from delaying."

Shina (HR Director): "But isn't it true that some companies delay just to avoid the headache of retraining employees?"

Gartner Analyst 2: "That's absolutely correct, Shina. Resistance to change is a common challenge. That's why early and comprehensive training is critical to minimize disruptions and improve adoption. Organisations that invest in their workforce during these transitions often see the highest ROI."

Albert Reynolds: "How do you recommend handling employee pushback? Or better yet, how do you convince IT staff that 'turning it off and on again' won't fix a TANA migration issue?"

Gartner Analyst 2 (smirking): "Great question. While that trick works on printers, migrating to TANA requires a slightly more sophisticated toolkit. To win hearts and minds, involve staff early, provide hands-on training, and showcase the platform's benefits through quick wins."

Case Studies: Lessons from the Field

Gartner Analyst 1: "We've analysed two major companies that have embarked on BARK TANA migrations. Let me share their experiences."

Case Study 1: Pharmaceuticals Cooperative (Pharma Manufacturing, Co-op Model)

- ✓ **Revenue:** £6.8 billion
- ✓ **Migration Cost:** £280 million
- ✓ **Context:** Cooperative of 150+ regional pharma suppliers across Europe, merging six legacy ERP systems.
- ✓ **Challenges:**
  - Heavy customization across sites
  - Misalignment between field ops and finance
  - Low digital literacy outside of HQ
- ✓ **Outcome:**
  - 14-month delay due to lack of local change management
  - £65 million in rework tied to overlooked intercompany process flows

- ✓ **Lesson:** Without embedded business change teams at site level, centralised ERP deployments stall.

Case Study 2: VistaServe Pharma Logistics (B2B Pharma Distribution, High Compliance)

- ✓ **Revenue:** £3.5 billion
- ✓ **Migration Cost:** £195 million
- ✓ **Context:** Operates across 45 global facilities, managing pharmaceutical distribution to healthcare providers under strict regulatory compliance.
- ✓ **Success Factors:**
  - Piloted BARK TANA across 4 tier-2 airport hubs before scaling
  - Digitised compliance tracking through real-time workflows
- ✓ **Outcome:**
  - Met regulatory KPIs within 6 months
  - 22% reduction in data latency for scheduling and inventory
- ✓ **Lesson:** When regulatory workflows are integrated early into the ERP design, time-to-value accelerates dramatically.

Burt (COO of KIP): "So, are you saying that process redesign is non-negotiable?"

Gartner Analyst 1: "Exactly. Migration isn't just an IT project—it's an organisational transformation. Investing upfront in aligning processes with the capabilities of TANA can save millions in long-term operational inefficiencies."

Alistair (CEO of KCP): "What happens if we skip testing altogether? Surely real-time analytics will fix any mistakes post-deployment, right?"

Gartner Analyst 2 (raising an eyebrow): "Skipping testing? Only if you want to experience real-time regret."

Q&A: Addressing Leadership Concerns

Prita Patel (GCFO): "What's the worst-case scenario for companies that don't migrate in time?"

Gartner Analyst 2: "Prita, the risks are significant: escalating support costs, inability to leverage advanced analytics, and reduced agility in responding to market demands. Organisations also risk falling behind competitors who embrace TANA's full potential."

Shina (HR Director): "How do we ensure internal alignment on such a complex initiative?"

Gartner Analyst 1: "Shina, alignment starts with communication. Create a cross-functional steering committee with representatives from IT, operations, finance, and key business units. Regular updates and transparent discussions about risks and progress are essential."

Peter (CISO): "And what about cybersecurity? Will TANA's native tools handle this, or do we need additional layers?"

Gartner Analyst 1: "TANA does offer robust native tools, but no single platform is a silver bullet. Always layer security tools to ensure comprehensive coverage. Think of it like locking your front door but also installing a camera and an alarm."

Closing Remarks by Gartner Analysts

Gartner Analyst 1: "Migration to BARK TANA is undoubtedly challenging, but it's an opportunity to rethink and future-proof your organisation. Start small, prioritize communication, and build alignment across all levels of the business."

Gartner Analyst 2: "Remember, the road to TANA isn't just about technology. It's about positioning your business to thrive in an increasingly competitive and data-driven world. The cost of inaction far outweighs the challenges of migration."

Scene Transition: Boardroom Discussion Post-Presentation

Alistair (CEO of KCP): "It's clear we can't ignore this, but we need a plan that minimizes risks. Let's assemble a task force to evaluate our readiness and start defining the first phase."

Prita Patel (GCFO): "Agreed. We need a detailed risk assessment and phased roadmap before committing to anything."

Albert Reynolds (European CEO): "Let's ensure we learn from these case studies. Marcus and I will work closely to draft the proposal for this task force and outline the initial stages. We need everyone's support to move forward efficiently."

As the discussion reached its peak, the CEO of KIP leaned back and spoke.

CEO of KIP: "I get the frustration, but we're talking about major operational changes. Are we really prepared to ignore industry advice due to perceived savings without any safeguards?"

The Group CFO hesitated before responding: "If this goes wrong, the cost won't just be financial—it'll be reputational. We need something—anything—that ensures accountability."

Marcus smiled thinly: "We either act now or remain stuck. We don't have time for hesitation."

Slowly, the room leaned in favour of his plan.

As Marcus prepared for the EXCO meeting, an emergency IT leadership call took place.

Group CIO: "We have to escalate this. If these governance changes go through without safeguards, we won't be able to manage risks."

The Service Delivery Manager shook his head: "We need to present alternatives—but they're shutting us out."

Before they could act, an email notification appeared, reading: "Final decision to be made by EXCO. No further IT input required."

The meeting room fell silent. The battle had been lost before it had even begun.

Private EXCO Discussion: Transition to BARK TANA

EXCO Q&A

The Private Meeting: A Divided Strategy

The EXCO members of the KIP and KCP businesses convened for a high-stakes private meeting, joined by Marcus and the COO of KCP Europe. The air was heavy with anticipation, as this session was set to determine the future of their BARK TANA migration strategy. While Marcus and the COO of Europe appeared confident, the GCFO harboured reservations, fuelled by conflicting data from TY and Gartner studies.

Before the final decision, Peter called an emergency IT meeting.

Peter: "We can't let this happen without a fight," he said firmly. "If these changes go through, security risks will spiral out of control."

Mark (Infrastructure Manager) nodded: "Then we need to escalate. If the leadership won't listen to reason, we must make sure they understand the consequences."

But before they could take action, the announcement came through—Marcus's plan had already been approved.

As the EXCO meeting began, the IT leadership team made one last attempt to intervene.

Service Delivery Manager: "We can't just approve this without an operational review. If we don't prepare for integration risks, we're setting ourselves up for disaster."

The Infrastructure Manager added: "This timeline is unrealistic—no team can execute this without shortcuts that will cost us later."

But the doors had already closed, and their voices faded behind them. The decision was happening, with or without them.

Opening Statements

Marcus: "Thank you all for making time today. As you know, we have an incredible opportunity before us to transition to BARK TANA swiftly and efficiently. Based on my experience and the relationships we've cultivated, I am pleased to share that we can deliver this migration for a total cost of £15 million and within six months. This is a game-changer for us."

COO of KCP Europe: "That's right. We've worked closely to ensure this plan addresses our operational needs without the excessive costs often quoted in industry studies. TCR, a trusted partner, has agreed to deliver the migration for £10 million. The remaining budget accounts for internal efforts and system enhancements."

GCFO's Concerns

GCFO: "I must admit, I'm struggling to reconcile this proposal with the figures we've seen from TY and Gartner. TY conducted a thorough four-month study for us, quoting a cost of £100-120 million. Gartner's industry benchmarks also point to a minimum of £150-250 million for a migration of this scale. How can we justify such a significant discrepancy?"

The room remained silent for a moment.

The GCFO exhaled. "Marcus, I've seen deals collapse because the numbers looked too good to be true. How can we be certain we're not setting ourselves up for financial failure?"

Albert Reynolds crossed his arms. "We've been in these rooms before. I've learned that when something seems this easy, it usually isn't."

The CEO of KIP hesitated before speaking: "We either take the risk or watch our competitors move first."

Slowly, the resistance began to fade.

Marcus (smiling): "I completely understand your concerns, but those figures are based on traditional approaches. TCR has offered us a bespoke solution leveraging their expertise and streamlined methodologies. They've worked with companies of similar size and achieved success at a fraction of the usual cost."

COO of KIP: "The TY study was overly conservative, in my opinion. We need to move decisively. The £15 million figure Marcus has secured represents a tremendous opportunity to unlock TANA's potential without burdening the company financially."

A Calculated Push

GCFO (leaning forward): "But this doesn't address the risks we've seen in other cases. Companies that underestimated migration costs faced spiralling expenses, operational disruptions, and long delays. If this plan is so unique, why hasn't it been widely adopted?"

COO of KCP Europe: "It's not about widespread adoption—it's about relationships and trust. Marcus's partnership with TCR gives us access to terms others can't achieve. Plus, the industry examples you reference involved poor management and outdated methodologies."

Marcus: "Exactly. With me leading this initiative, I can ensure that we avoid the pitfalls others have encountered. By eliminating unnecessary complexities and focusing on what truly matters, we can achieve a seamless transition."

Albert Reynolds looked around the table. "Marcus, I need more than just confidence. We're committing to a major structural shift, and I can't sign off without understanding the real-world risks."

The CEO of KIP tapped his fingers against the table: "I still think this is rushed. If it fails, we'll be the ones explaining it to the board."

The room remained silent for a long moment before Marcus leaned forward. "We either act now or lose the opportunity entirely. There is no safe option here—only forward."

Slowly, the resistance faded.

The CEOs Weigh In

CEO of KCP: "I've heard both sides, and I must say, the cost and timeline Marcus proposes are incredibly compelling. If we delay, we risk paying exponentially more in extended support costs. The Gartner report may provide useful insights, but it's not tailored to our unique situation."

CEO of KIP: "I agree. We can't afford to waste time debating when we have a clear path forward. In the first instance it doesn't affect my business so Marcus, you have my support. Let's move ahead with the £15 million plan."

GCFO (frowning): "I'm not convinced. TY's findings are based on proven methodologies. This deal seems too good to be true. We're overlooking the long-term implications of underestimating such a complex migration."

COO of KCP Europe (leaning back confidently): "We understand your reservations, but the majority of us see this as an opportunity we can't ignore. Delays will only cost us more."

Additional Deliberations

GCFO: "Before we proceed, I'd like us to revisit the TY study. They outlined clear risks related to business process reengineering, data migration complexity, and integration with legacy systems. Are we prepared to handle these challenges within the proposed budget?"

Marcus (interrupting): "We've accounted for all these factors. TCR has already delivered similar projects and assures us that their methodology minimizes disruptions. Their success rate speaks for itself."

GCFO: "But Gartner also highlighted issues with underestimating testing timelines and organisational readiness. How do we address these without increasing costs?"

COO of KIP: "Gartner's findings are broad strokes based on averages. What we're discussing here is a tailored solution. Let's not get bogged down by generic scenarios."

CEO of KCP: "Agreed. The numbers from TY and Gartner are useful, but they don't reflect Marcus's specific plan. I trust his expertise and the COO's confidence in this approach."

GCFO: "Trust is important, but data and precedent are critical. This isn't a decision we can reverse if it goes wrong. We're discussing millions in cost reductions, but we have yet to see a detailed breakdown of expenses. If these projections are wrong, we could face budget overruns that wipe out any perceived savings. This is a financial risk we can't afford to overlook."

Marcus gave a tight-lipped smile and spoke firmly: "We've accounted for everything. Let's not get caught up in unnecessary concerns. It's time to act. This is why I'm leading the charge. We'll ensure this is a success, and I'll personally oversee every step."

Prita pulled Richard aside after the meeting and admitted: "Something about this doesn't sit right. Marcus makes bold claims, but he hasn't shown real evidence yet."

Richard frowned: "I agree, but we don't have a better option. If he's right, we'll look like fools for holding his back."

As the discussion wrapped up, Prita hesitated: "Marcus, I need more than just your word. If this goes wrong, I'll be the one justifying it to the board."

Richard frowned, exchanging a look with the Group CFO. "This is a huge risk. We need something more concrete before signing off."

But before doubts could settle, Marcus leaned in: "We can sit here debating risks, or we can act. If we delay, we lose leverage."

Slowly, the hesitation faded.

The Vote

COO of KCP Europe: "Let's put it to a vote. We've heard the arguments. Those in favour of proceeding with the £15 million plan?"

CEO of KCP: "Yes."

CEO of KIP: "Yes."

GCFO: "No."

COO of KCP Europe: "The majority have spoken. Marcus, you have the green light. Please proceed and keep us updated."

Aftermath

As the meeting adjourned, the GCFO remained uneasy. Despite being outvoted, she resolved to monitor the project closely, suspecting that the £15 million promise would unravel under scrutiny. Meanwhile, Marcus and the COO of Europe exchanged satisfied glances. Their plan to sideline the GCIO and push the initiative through had succeeded, setting the stage for what could either be a groundbreaking success or a catastrophic misstep.

The leadership team's decision to override IT security wasn't just a miscalculation—it was classic cognitive dissonance. Faced with evidence contradicting their vision, they doubled down, preferring Marcus's optimism over operational reality.

Closing Thought

The decision exemplified the tension between ambition and prudence. While the promise of rapid transformation at minimal cost was alluring, the shadow of scepticism lingered. Time would reveal whether Marcus's confidence was well-placed or another chapter in the annals of overconfidence gone awry.

Chapter Five

Beyond Belief

Why Do We Believe?

In the realm of IT and beyond, the question arises: why do people favour believing lies, even when evidence conspicuously contradicts them? It's a peculiar facet of human nature that transcends the boundaries of logic and reason, with profound implications for decision-making in high-stakes environments. This phenomenon is not limited to specific sectors; it manifests across industries, often leading to costly and avoidable failures.

Psychologists have long studied the human psyche, unravelling the intricate tapestry of our beliefs and biases. These tendencies are particularly magnified in the corporate world, where complexity and pressure drive individuals toward cognitive shortcuts. Leaders, faced with overwhelming data and time constraints, often gravitate toward convenient narratives. The intersection of psychology, industry pressures, and decision-making exposes a stark reality: organisations often perpetuate myths, favouring comfort over truth. This behaviour is not just a quirk of human nature, but a systemic issue embedded within corporate culture.

Dr. Daniel Kahneman and Cognitive Biases

Dr. Daniel Kahneman, a Nobel laureate in economics sciences, has profoundly shaped our understanding of human decision-making. His research into heuristics—mental shortcuts used under uncertainty—illustrates why people often fall prey to confirmation bias. This tendency to favour information that supports preexisting beliefs, while ignoring contradictory evidence, is especially prevalent in IT and other complex environments.

For example, in BARK TANA migration projects, leaders may dismiss warnings from experienced stakeholders if those warnings challenge their optimistic assumptions. The allure of projected cost savings and speed often overshadows the intricate realities of system integration, creating an environment ripe for flawed strategies to take root. This dynamic is not confined to IT; in manufacturing, similar biases lead to underestimating the challenges of automating production lines, resulting in operational bottlenecks and financial overruns.

Dr. Elizabeth Loftus and the Malleability of Memory

Dr. Elizabeth Loftus, a renowned psychologist, has demonstrated that human memory is reconstructive rather than static. Her work reveals how memories can be influenced by misinformation, leading individuals to recall events inaccurately. In IT projects, this phenomenon often manifests as stakeholders misremembering past successes, portraying them as smoother and less costly than they truly were. This distorted narrative bolsters unrealistic expectations for new initiatives, perpetuating a cycle of overpromising and underdelivering.

Industries like healthcare face similar challenges. Hospital administrators might recall AI diagnostic tools as delivering seamless improvements, overlooking the extensive staff training and system integration required. These selective memories shape future decisions, compounding errors and eroding trust.

The Dunning-Kruger Effect

The Dunning-Kruger effect, identified by psychologists David Dunning and Justin Kruger, highlights a paradox: individuals with limited knowledge often overestimate their competence. In the corporate world, this overconfidence can have disastrous consequences. For instance, an executive with a superficial understanding of cloud migrations might champion a project timeline that seasoned IT professionals know is unattainable. This disconnects between perceived and actual expertise frequently leads to costly missteps.

Similar patterns emerge in financial services. Leaders, enamoured with the promise of blockchain technology, might push for its rapid adoption without fully understanding compliance requirements or integration challenges. Overconfidence, fuelled by partial knowledge, undermines not only project success but also organisational credibility.

The Dunning-Kruger effect describes a cognitive bias where individuals with limited knowledge or competence in a particular domain overestimate their abilities. Marcus's confidence in his BARK TANA migration plan was a textbook case. He dismissed experts, ignored warnings, and assumed he understood the full complexity of enterprise migrations—despite evidence to the contrary. It was Dunning-Kruger in real time. This phenomenon has led to notable missteps in the corporate world, where leaders' overconfidence, stemming from insufficient understanding, has resulted in significant failures.

Case Study: WeWork's Overexpansion

A prominent example is the rapid expansion strategy of WeWork under co-founder Adam Neumann. Neumann, with limited experience in commercial real estate, aggressively scaled the company's operations, believing that WeWork could revolutionize the office space industry. This overconfidence led to overexpansion, financial instability, and a failed initial public offering (IPO), culminating in Neumann's resignation and a drastic devaluation of the company. Case Study: Pets.com's Market Misjudgement

Another instance involves Pets.com, an online pet supply retailer founded by Greg McLemore. McLemore, coming from a background in children's toys, assumed that selling pet supplies online would mirror his previous ventures. This misjudgement of the market dynamics, coupled with overconfidence in the business model, led to the company's collapse within a year, resulting in significant financial losses.

Case Study: McArthur Wheeler's Bank Robberies

An illustrative, albeit extreme, example is the case of McArthur Wheeler, who, in 1995, robbed two banks without any disguise, believing that rubbing lemon juice on his skin would render him invisible to security cameras. This misguided belief stemmed from a profound misunderstanding of basic scientific principles, leading to his swift arrest. This incident directly inspired the research into the Dunning-Kruger effect.

Real-world Implications in IT

In IT, the rapid pace of technological advancement and the sheer volume of data can overwhelm even experienced professionals. This often results in decision-makers "switching off" and defaulting to simplified narratives that align with their emotional comfort zones. It's easier to accept a plausible lie—such as the promise of a rapid, low-cost BARK TANA migration—than to delve into the complexities that might refute it.

External pressures further compound this issue. Prita Patel's objections in Chapter 3 were a perfect example of this resistance. Even when faced with data contradicting Marcus's claims, key executives preferred the easier narrative of cost savings and speed. This resistance fosters an environment where lies flourish, perpetuating cycles of inefficiency and financial loss. The IT sector, with its intricate systems and evolving technologies, serves as a microcosm for these challenges.

Emotional Security and Cognitive Dissonance

The acceptance of falsehoods often stems from the interplay between emotional security and cognitive dissonance. When confronted with facts that challenge deeply held beliefs, individuals experience discomfort. To alleviate this cognitive dissonance, they may reject new evidence and cling to narratives that reinforce their worldview.

This tendency transcends industries. In manufacturing, for instance, leaders might downplay the operational disruptions associated with a new production system, favouring optimistic timelines despite evidence from peer companies. Similarly, in healthcare, executives might underestimate the challenges of adopting electronic health records, ignoring warnings from early adopters about integration difficulties and staff resistance. Across sectors, cognitive dissonance creates a barrier to embracing inconvenient truths.

Industries and Capabilities

The patterns explored here are not unique to IT. Across industries, the gap between optimism and realism persists:

- ✓ Manufacturing: Overpromised savings from automation projects lead to misaligned production schedules and resource strains. Leaders often ignore logistical hurdles, resulting in delayed rollouts and unexpected costs.
- ✓ Healthcare: Administrators might embrace AI diagnostics without adequately training staff or addressing data privacy concerns, undermining patient care and regulatory compliance.
- ✓ Financial Services: The rush to adopt blockchain solutions often overlooks compliance, scalability, and integration complexities. These oversights result in fragmented systems and unmet promises.

This widespread phenomenon underscores a critical capability gap in leadership: the ability to discern truth from convenience. Effective leaders must cultivate an environment where evidence-based decision-making prevails over emotional or reputational considerations. By prioritizing transparency and fostering a culture of accountability, organisations can bridge this gap and align their strategies with achievable outcomes.

Conclusion

The human psyche's propensity to believe lies stems from a complex interplay of cognitive biases, emotional comfort, and the difficulty of processing intricate information. By understanding these underlying factors and fostering a culture of transparency and critical thinking, organisations can mitigate the risks of misinformation.

Addressing these challenges requires leaders to recognise their own cognitive biases, engage with diverse perspectives, and ground decisions in robust evidence. Only then can they navigate the treacherous waters of misinformation and build resilient, informed organisations.

Next Chapter Preview

In the next chapter, we will explore the Veritus Model, a simple framework designed to help organisations identify and counter misinformation. This practical tool will empower leaders to make decisions rooted in data, ensuring sustainable success.

Had the ASRM (Veritus Model) framework been applied, the leadership team would have identified the lack of financial benchmarking (Alignment), questioned Marcus's unverified claims (Stakeholder Engagement), and realised the risk of cost overruns (Risk & Reward Assessment). Instead, they acted on instinct—and the consequences were inevitable.

Chapter Six

Rebuke Overconfident Persuaders with Veritus

Time to Change

Introducing the Reality Check Framework for Senior Leaders

Veritus = Alignment, Stakeholders, Risk/ Reward, Motive – ASRM

Guiding Decision-Making with Clarity and Confidence

Had the ASRM framework been applied, the leadership team would have flagged the misalignment of BARK cost estimates (Alignment), questioned Marcus's unverified claims (Stakeholder Engagement), and realised the risk of cost overruns (Risk & Reward Assessment). Instead, they acted on instinct—and the consequences were inevitable.

In our journey to enhance organisational success and resilience, it is imperative to adopt structured approaches that assist senior leaders in making informed decisions. If this framework had been applied in Chapter 3's BARK TANA decision, it would have flagged the misalignment of cost estimates early, ensuring that the business didn't blindly follow Marcus's version of events.

The Challenge

In leadership, it is not uncommon to encounter decisions fuelled more by ego and overconfidence than by solid evidence. Such decision-making can lead to profound consequences, resulting in significant financial and reputational costs. The Reality Check Framework seeks to address these challenges head-on, ensuring that each decision is anchored in reality and aligned with the organisation's best interests.

The Solution: Reality Check Framework

This framework is uncomplicated and practical, offering a step-by-step guide to help senior leaders validate claims, engage stakeholders, and assess risks versus rewards. It is designed to ruffle feathers, as it demands a rigorous commitment to truth and transparency—a necessity in today's fast-paced and competitive business environment.

Step 1: Alignment with Evidence

Purpose: Validate the credibility of the claim or proposal.
Define the Claim or Proposal: Clearly articulate the key promise or objective (e.g., cost savings, timeline, expected benefits).
Gather Benchmark Data: Review historical data, industry standards, and case studies of similar initiatives.

Step 2: Stakeholder Engagement

Purpose: Ensure all relevant parties are involved and their insights are considered.
Identify Key Stakeholders: Determine who will be impacted by the decision and who has valuable input.
Facilitate Open Communication: Encourage honest discussions and feedback from all stakeholders.

Step 3: Risk vs. Reward Assessment

Purpose: Evaluate the potential benefits against the possible risks.
Analyse Potential Outcomes: Consider best-case and worst-case scenarios and their probabilities.
Weigh Risks and Rewards: Decide whether the potential benefits justify the risks involved.

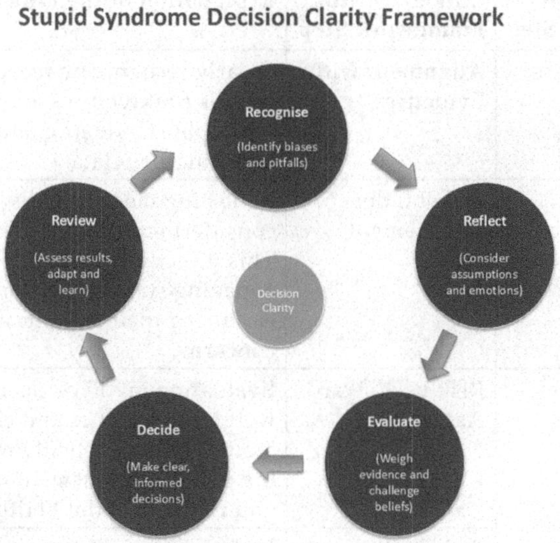

Figure 1: The Stupid Syndrome Decision Clarity Framework—supporting clearer decision-making by recognising cognitive biases and avoiding common leadership pitfalls.

Now that we've visually outlined our Decision Clarity Framework, let's explicitly explore how it integrates with our detailed Veritus Reality Check model.

Step 4: Motive & Incentive Check (NEW)

Who benefits personally from signature vs successful go-live?
Are there EOQ/FY pressures, SPIFFs, or bonus triggers?
Is accountability tied to outcomes (stability, quality, ROI) or to contracted savings?

How the Decision Clarity Framework Aligns to the Veritus (Reality Check) Model

The Decision Clarity Framework (Recognise, Reflect, Evaluate, Decide, Review) provides a clear, intuitive cycle to guide leaders through critical decision points. It directly aligns and integrates

Decision Clarity Step	Linked Veritus Framework Step	Explanation of the Link
Recognise	Alignment with Evidence	Clearly recognizing biases and pitfalls first requires alignment with robust evidence and benchmarked data.
Reflect	Stakeholder Engagement	Reflecting means clearly considering different perspectives. This directly links to actively engaging stakeholders and capturing their insights and concerns.
Evaluate	Risk vs. Reward Assessment	Evaluating involves clearly weighing evidence and challenging assumptions, explicitly matching the detailed assessment of risks and rewards in the Veritus model.
Decide	Risk vs. Reward Assessment	Making clear, informed decisions explicitly follows from a thorough evaluation, considering outcomes explicitly assessed in the risk vs. reward step.
Review	Alignment, Stakeholder, Risk & Reward *(Iterative reflection)*	Reviewing outcomes means explicitly revisiting the evidence, stakeholder feedback, and risk vs. reward assumptions made, reinforcing a continuous, iterative cycle of clarity and improvement.

with the detailed, structured steps of the Veritus Reality Check Framework as follows:

Conclusion

By implementing the Reality Check Framework, senior leaders can navigate decision-making processes with greater confidence and clarity. This framework not only aids in identifying truth from falsehood but also fosters a culture of accountability and evidence-based decisions. While it may challenge existing norms and egos, it is a crucial step towards sustainable organisational success.

Remember, life is full of feathers, and sometimes they need to be ruffled to reveal the truth and pave the way for progress.

Step-by-Step Guide: Reality Check Framework (Veritus Framework)

Introduction

The Reality Check Framework is a practical, structured approach for executives to assess and make informed decisions. This guide breaks the process into four key steps—Alignment with Evidence, Stakeholder Engagement, Risk vs Reward Assessment, and Motive & Incentive Check—ensuring a robust decision-making process.

Step 1: Alignment with Evidence

Purpose: Validate the credibility of the claim or proposal.

- Define the Claim or Proposal:
- Clearly articulate the key promise or objective (e.g., cost savings, timeline, expected benefits).

Gather Benchmark Data:

- Review historical data, industry standards, and case studies of similar initiatives.
- Identify deviations between the proposal and known benchmarks.

Assess Credibility:

- Validate the sources of information to ensure they are reliable (e.g., internal experts, reputable consultants).

Action:

- Proceed: If evidence strongly supports the claim.
- Reassess: If gaps or unrealistic assumptions exist.
- Reject: Evidence is weak or contradictory; do not proceed.

Step 2: Stakeholder Engagement

Purpose: Gather input from key stakeholders to build consensus and address concerns.

Identify Key Stakeholders:

- Include domain experts, team leads, and those directly impacted by the decision.

Solicit Feedback:

- Use meetings, surveys, or one-on-one discussions to collect input.
- Categorize feedback into:
  1. Supportive
  2. Neutral
  3. Opposed

Evaluate Concerns:

- Document significant concerns or red flags raised by stakeholders.
- Work to address areas of disagreement.

Action:

- Proceed: If most stakeholders support the decision.
- Reassess: If significant opposition arises.

Step 3: Risk vs. Reward Assessment

Purpose: Analyse potential risks and benefits to ensure balanced decision-making.

Identify Potential Risks:

- List risks such as financial overrun, operational challenges, reputational damage, or regulatory impacts.

Analyse Risks:

- Use a risk matrix to categorize:
  - Low Impact: Minimal disruption.

- Medium Impact: Manageable but requires mitigation plans.
- High Impact: Severe consequences.

Assess Rewards:

- Evaluate tangible and intangible benefits (e.g., cost savings, competitive advantage, improved efficiency).
- Weigh rewards against risks.

Action:

- Proceed — Risks are manageable and well-mitigated.
- Reassess — Adjustments needed to reduce risk.
- Reject — Risks outweigh potential benefits.

Step 4: Motive & Incentive Check

Purpose:

- Expose personal/organisational incentives that bias the decision toward signing now rather than successful outcomes.

Questions:

- Who benefits personally at signature vs go-live (bonus, SPIFFs, promotion, equity, vendor ties)?
- Any EOQ/FY pressure or expiring discounts shaping the timeline?
- Are acceptance and payments tied to operational outcomes (stability, quality, ROI) vs "booked savings"?
- Are key personnel named & locked, with replacement-approval and service-credit terms?

Action (gate):

- Proceed — Motives transparent and aligned to outcomes; 60–90-day price-hold in place; named-personnel lock; outcome-based acceptance/holdbacks agreed.

- Reassess – Motives partly opaque or EOQ pressure unresolved; renegotiate incentives/clauses and re-run Step 1.
- Reject – Motives opaque/misaligned; refusal to disclose conflicts or align incentives.

Decision Points

Proceed:

- Greenlight the initiative if evidence aligns, stakeholders support, and risks are manageable.
- Develop a monitoring plan to track progress and adjust if necessary.

Reassess:

- Pause and reevaluate if evidence is weak, stakeholders are divided, or risks outweigh rewards.
- Gather additional data, adjust the plan, or delay the decision until confidence improves.

Reject:

- Decision is not viable; explore alternatives.

Tips for Effective Implementation

Document Findings:

- Maintain a summary of evidence, stakeholder input, and risk assessments for transparency.

Communicate Regularly:

- Share updates with stakeholders to maintain alignment and manage expectations.

Review Periodically:

- Revisit the decision after key milestones to ensure continued alignment with goals.

Summary

The Reality Check Framework provides a simple yet powerful tool for executives to navigate complex decisions with clarity and confidence. By following these steps, organisations can ensure their choices are informed, collaborative, and resilient against risks.

Worked Example: Applying the Step-by-Step Guide

Introduction

The Reality Check Framework is a practical, structured approach for executives to assess and make informed decisions. This guide breaks the process into four key steps—Alignment with Evidence, Stakeholder Engagement, Risk vs Reward Assessment, and Motive & Incentive Check.

Step 1: Alignment with Evidence

Purpose: Validate the credibility of the claim or proposal.

Define the Claim or Proposal:

- Proposal: Migrate BARK to BARK TANA within 6 months at a cost of £15 million.

Gather Benchmark Data:

- Historical Data: Similar migrations documented in industry reports and Gartner briefings indicate that such projects take a minimum of 1 year and cost upwards of £100 million.
- Case Studies: Examples from the book's chapters include:

    1. A £280 million BARK migration project at a major pharmaceutical company ("Pharmaceuticals Cooperative").
    2. A £195 million project involving extensive business process changes ("VistaServe Pharma Logistics").

Assess Credibility:

- Sources include feedback from Gartner and other companies that have undertaken similar migrations.
- The claim contradicts documented benchmarks, signalling potential misinformation.

Action:

- Reassess: The proposal's timeline and cost are unrealistic compared to historical data.

Step 2: Stakeholder Engagement

Purpose: Gather input from key stakeholders to build consensus and address concerns.

Identify Key Stakeholders:

- Marcus (Proposer of the migration)
- Graham (CTO with 30 years of IT experience)
- Business Leaders from North America and Europe

2.1: Solicit Feedback:

Stakeholder Inputs:

- Marcus insists on the feasibility of the proposal based on vendor assurances.
- Graham raises concerns, citing system complexities and previous migration experiences.
- Business leaders express urgency but lack technical understanding.

Evaluate Concerns:

- Concerns include:
  - Insufficient testing time.
  - Overlooking complexities such as business data integration and finance system changes.
  - Risk of overspending due to unanticipated issues.

Action:

- Reassess: Significant stakeholder opposition, especially from the experienced CTO, warrants revisiting the proposal.

Step 3: Risk vs. Reward Assessment

Purpose: Analyse potential risks and benefits to ensure balanced decision-making.

Identify Potential Risks:

- Financial Risk: Actual costs could exceed £100 million, far beyond the £15 million estimate.
- Operational Risk: Critical disruptions due to incomplete testing or rushed implementation.
- Reputational Risk: Failure could undermine leadership credibility and stakeholder trust.

Analyse Risks:

- High likelihood of overspending and project delays.
- Potential for long-term operational inefficiencies if the migration is not properly executed.

Assess Rewards:

- Benefits of migration include improved scalability, real-time analytics, and operational efficiency.
- Rewards are contingent on proper execution, making the unrealistic timeline a critical barrier.

Action:

- Proceed – Risks are manageable and well-mitigated.
- Reassess – Adjustments needed to reduce risk.
- Reject – Risks outweigh potential benefits.

Step 4: Motive & Incentive Check

Purpose:

- Expose personal/organisational incentives that bias the decision toward signing now rather than successful outcomes.

Questions:

- Who benefits personally at signature vs go-live (bonus, SPIFFs, promotion, equity, vendor ties)?
- Any EOQ/FY pressure or expiring discounts shaping the timeline?
- Are acceptance and payments tied to operational outcomes (stability, quality, ROI) vs "booked savings"?
- Are key personnel named & locked with replacement-approval and service-credit terms?

Action (gate):

- Proceed – Motives transparent and aligned to outcomes; 60–90-day price-hold in place; named-personnel lock; outcome-based acceptance/holdbacks agreed.
- Reassess – Motives partly opaque or EOQ pressure unresolved; renegotiate incentives/clauses and re-run Step 1.
- Reject – Motives opaque/misaligned; refusal to disclose conflicts or align incentives.

Decision Points

Proceed:

- Only feasible with a revised timeline and realistic cost projections aligned with stakeholder input and historical data.

Reassess:

- Reevaluate the proposal with input from experts, adjusted timelines, and comprehensive risk mitigation strategies.

Reject:

- Decision is not viable; explore alternatives.

Tips for Effective Implementation

Document Findings:

- The evidence from the chapters underscores the need for thorough benchmarking and stakeholder engagement.

Communicate Regularly:

- Transparency in addressing unrealistic expectations is critical to maintaining trust.

Review Periodically:

- Reassess at key project milestones to ensure alignment with goals and adapt as necessary.

Summary

Applying the Reality Check Framework to the BARK TANA migration proposal reveals critical gaps in evidence, stakeholder alignment, and risk assessment. By following this structured approach, leadership can make informed decisions, avoid costly errors and ensure project success.

Reality Check Framework (Veritus Model) – Action Plan

Use this structured template to assess decisions, validate assumptions, and navigate leadership challenges effectively.

Step 1: Alignment with Evidence

Define the Key Decision or Claim:

Motive & EOQ Red-Flags

Signature-based bonuses (presenter/vendor) → Defer until acceptance is outcome-based (stability/quality/ROI), not signature.

EOQ/FY expiring price → demand 60–90-day price hold + decide after an independent estimate.

SOW gap (change, testing, data cleansing, hypercare missing) → Stop; require line-item inclusions.

Incomparable references → run apples-to-apples scope compare + call the delivery lead (not sales).

(Example: "We can complete our IT transformation in 6 months with minimal risk.")

Gather Supporting Evidence:

What historical data, case studies, or industry benchmarks validate this claim?

Does this align with past experiences in the company or industry?

Are there gaps or inconsistencies in the available data?

Decision for this Step:

- ☐ Proceed – The claim is well-supported.
- ☐ Reassess – More validation is needed.
- ☐ Reject – The claim lacks credible evidence.

Step 2: Stakeholder Engagement

Identify Key Stakeholders:

Who are the experts, influencers, and decision-makers involved?

Who stands to benefit or be impacted by this decision?

Is there broad agreement, or are there critical objections?

Decision for this Step:

- ☐ Proceed – Stakeholders are aligned.
- ☐ Reassess – Key objections require resolution.
- ☐ Reject – Stakeholder concerns indicate high risk.

Step 3: Risk vs. Reward Assessment

Identify and Weigh Risks:

What financial, operational, and reputational risks exist?

What is the worst-case scenario if things go wrong?

Decision for this Step:

- □ Proceed – Risks are manageable and well-mitigated.
- □ Reassess – Adjustments needed to reduce risk.
- □ Reject – Risks outweigh potential benefits.

Step 4: Motive & Incentive Check Document presenter incentives (bonus, promotion, equity, supplier ties).

Require contract clauses that align incentives to outcomes, not signatures.

Decision for this Step:

- □ Proceed – Motives disclosed; incentives aligned to outcomes; price-hold in place; named-personnel lock; outcome-based acceptance/holdbacks agreed.
- □ Reassess – Partial disclosure or unresolved EOQ pressure; renegotiate incentives/clauses.
- □ Reject – Motives opaque/misaligned; refusal to align incentives or disclose conflicts.

Final Decision Summary

Proceed – Move forward with confidence.

Reassess – Adjust plan and revalidate.

Reject – Decision is not viable; explore alternatives.

Tip: Keep this worksheet visible in leadership discussions and revisit it for major business decisions.

Veritus Model: Decision Validation Worksheet (Example)

Throughout this chapter, we've clearly shown how visual, intuitive frameworks and detailed analytical models combine effectively to support robust decision-making. By explicitly aligning the Decision Clarity Framework with the Veritus (Reality Check) model, you now have practical tools to systematically identify biases, engage stakeholders constructively, evaluate risks accurately, and ultimately make clear, evidence-based decisions. As you move forward, keep this structured approach close at hand—ensuring your organisation's choices remain anchored in reality.

Section 1: Presenter Motives & Bias

1.	**Is the presenter's primary motive clearly stated and transparent? -** Explicitly stated intentions and goals. What do they gain from this activity. Clearly document if the presenter is directly incentivized through bonuses, career advancement, or equity arrangements tied explicitly to the recommendation.	[Answers Y or N & Your Notes]
2.	**Does the presenter have a clear incentive aligned with accuracy and truthfulness? -** Clear incentives (financial, reputational, ethical) supporting accuracy. What do they gain from starting. How are they linked to the outcome? Do they start something then leave for better role. Do they know the party personally or has there been a fair evaluation or just a promise. Check personal or organisational histories. Has the presenter repeatedly recommended certain solutions, vendors, or approaches previously, and how successful have those recommendations historically been?	[Answers Y or N & Your Notes]
3.	**Has the presenter explicitly acknowledged potential biases or conflicts of interest? -** Transparent discussion of personal, professional, and financial biases.	[Answers Y or N & Your Notes]
4.	**Is there evidence that the presenter has previously provided accurate and reliable information? -** Historical review of presenter's reliability and accuracy. Not a face value search but a find people that may have worked with the person previously that would be critical of them	[Answers Y or N & Your Notes]

5.	**Are any quarter-end or year-end accelerators disclosed?**	[Answers Y or N & Your Notes]
6.	**Are the core assumptions behind the claim clearly identified?** - Assumptions explicitly listed and detailed without ambiguity.	[Answers Y or N & Your Notes]

Section 2: Assumption Validation

7.	**Have these assumptions been independently verified?** - External, independent verification by a trusted third party. Do they align to the presenters' recommendations. Consider checking alignment with industry standards, benchmarks, or regulatory compliance standards relevant to your business.	[Answers Y or N & Your Notes]
8.	**Are there concrete data points or evidence supporting the assumptions?** - Tangible, quantifiable data or credible qualitative evidence provided. These should be from reputable sources. Include reference checks against historical performance or similar past projects within your organisation or sector. If a decision carries significant reputational or monetary risk, proactively reach out to organisations that have undertaken similar initiatives. Ask for their lessons learned and solicit balanced feedback on the credibility of the scenario you're evaluating.	[Answers Y or N & Your Notes]
9.	**Is there evidence demonstrating attempts to disprove or challenge these assumptions?** - Documented scenarios or tests challenging assumptions transparently shared.	[Answers Y or N & Your Notes]

Section 3: Information Reliability

10. **Has the information provided been corroborated by a second, independent source? -** Confirmation by at least one credible, independent source. It's better to get two independent sources on top of what is being presented	[Answers Y or N & Your Notes] (maximum of two)
11. **Is the source of the information generally regarded as credible? -** Reputation, expertise, and historical reliability of source verified. Differentiate clearly between primary sources (original data/reports) and secondary sources (commentaries/summaries); primary sources are typically more reliable.	[Answers Y or N & Your Notes]
12. **Have alternative explanations or contrary evidence been considered and adequately addressed? -** Open discussion and resolution of counterarguments and alternative explanations. Confirm if competitive analyses or market alternatives have been adequately explored and included.	[Answers Y or N & Your Notes]
13. **Is the information timely and relevant to the current context? -** Reflects most recent data and is directly applicable. This should be within the last 6 months as technology moves so quickly. Saying that you did something 4 years ago for 2million doesn't work with delivery these days	[Answers Y or N & Your Notes]

Section 4: Transparency and Hidden Agendas

14. **Have potential hidden agendas or conflicts of interest been explicitly discussed and resolved?** - Explicit acknowledgment and resolution of potential hidden motives or conflicts. – these could be previous partnerships or delivery. Comes back to running fair procurement against 3 companies if relating to delivery. Friends often will loosely underwrite deliveries yet contracted the person is not taking the risk from the recommendations. Check explicitly for hidden vendor or supplier relationships, including subcontracting or reciprocal business arrangements.	[Answers Y or N & Your Notes]

15. **Is there documented openness regarding the methodology used to arrive at the claim or recommendation? -** Methodology clearly explained and documented.	[Answers Y or N & Your Notes]
16. **Has the presenter encouraged questions and challenges openly from the audience or stakeholders**? - Active solicitation and responsiveness to questioning and challenges. Have these been addressed or pushed off into later, if the later then these need to be completed upfront. Evaluate not just whether challenges were encouraged but the quality of responses provided—were they thorough, factual, timely, and complete?	[Answers Y or N & Your Notes]
17. **Are there explicit guarantees or accountability mechanisms including acceptance tied to operational outcomes, defined holdbacks/ service credits, change-order caps, and any price-hold commitment? -** Explicit accountability mechanisms ensuring transparency and corrective actions. How do you link in a staff member or department. Normally you must change their yearly performance objectives and make it 80-90 percent waited on meeting milestones. Check if an escalation or dispute resolution process is clearly outlined, particularly regarding failed outcomes or missed milestones.	[Answers Y or N & Your Notes]

Additional Considerations for Senior Executives

18. **Financial Impact & Risk Exposure.** Has the presenter clearly outlined short-term and long-term financial implications, including total cost of ownership and clearly defined financial risk exposure?	[Answers Y or N & Your Notes]
19. **Implementation Capability & Track Record.** Does the presenter or recommended vendor clearly demonstrate past success in executing similarly scaled projects, including documented lessons learned from past challenges and are **key delivery personnel named & locked**, with **replacement approval** terms?	[Answers Y or N & Your Notes]

20. **Scalability & Futureproofing.** Is there explicit consideration of scalability and adaptability of the recommendation to future changes in market, regulation, or business strategy? Making sure you're not locked in for 3 years, and it prevents the company from pivoting.	[Answers Y or N & Your Notes]
21. **Senior Business Sponsorship and Accountability.** Is there a clearly identified senior responsible owner (SRO) from the business—not from the technical delivery side—to sponsor and advocate for the initiative? This individual should have significant authority and credibility within their division, ensuring the initiative remains strategically aligned with business objectives. Additionally, their division should have performance objectives explicitly linked to the success of the initiative, embedding organisational accountability rather than isolating it as solely a technical responsibility.	[Answers Y or N & Your Notes]

Scoring Interpretation:

- ✓ **16–21 (22 if you get two independent sources) Yes's:** Reliable evidence. Assumptions and motives are clear.
- ✓ **10–15 Yes's:** or Motives Fail: Caution advised. Recommend additional validation.
- ✓ **0–9 Yes's:** High risk. Strongly advise deeper investigation or reconsideration.

BUSINESS BOOKS

Business Books

Business Books publishes practical guides and insightful non-fiction for beginners and professionals. Covering aspects from management skills, leadership and organizational change to positive work environments, career coaching and self-care for managers, our books are a valuable addition to those working in the world of business.

15 Ways to Own Your Future

Take Control of Your Destiny in Business and in Life

Michael Khouri

A 15-point blueprint for creating better collaboration, enjoyment, and success in business and in life.

Paperback: 978-1-78535-300-0 ebook: 978-1-78535-301-7

The Common Excuses of the Comfortable Compromiser

Understanding Why People Oppose Your Great Idea

Matt Crossman

Comfortable compromisers block the way of anyone trying to change anything. This is your guide to their common excuses.

Paperback: 978-1-78099-595-3 ebook: 978-1-78099-596-0

The Failing Logic of Money

Duane Mullin

Money is wasteful and cruel, causes war, crime and dysfunctional feudalism. Humankind needs happiness, peace and abundance. So banish money and use technology and knowledge to rid the world of war, crime and poverty.

Paperback: 978-1-84694-259-4 ebook: 978-1-84694-888-6

Mastering the Mommy Track

Juggling Career and Kids in Uncertain Times

Erin Flynn Jay

Mastering the Mommy Track tells the stories of everyday working mothers, the challenges they have faced, and lessons learned.

Paperback: 978-1-78099-123-8 ebook: 978-1-78099-124-5

Modern Day Selling

Unlocking Your Hidden Potential

Brian Barfield

Learn how to reconnect sales associates with customers and unlock hidden sales potential.

Paperback: 978-1-78099-457-4 ebook: 978-1-78099-458-1

The Most Creative, Escape the Ordinary, Excel at Public Speaking Book Ever

All The Help You Will Ever Need in Giving a Speech

Philip Theibert

The 'everything you need to give an outstanding speech' book, complete with original material written by a professional speech-writer.

Paperback: 978-1-78099-672-1 ebook: 978-1-78099-673-8

On Business And For Pleasure

A Self-Study Workbook for Advanced Business English

Michael Berman

This workbook includes enjoyable challenges and has been designed to help students with the English they need for work.

Paperback: 978-1-84694-304-1

Small Change, Big Deal

Money as if People Mattered

Jennifer Kavanagh

Money is about relationships: between individuals and between communities. Small is still beautiful, as peer lending model, micro-credit, shows.

Paperback: 978-1-78099-313-3 ebook: 978-1-78099-314-0

Readers of ebooks can buy or view any of these bestsellers by clicking on the live link in the title. Most titles are published in paperback and as an ebook. Paperbacks are available in traditional bookshops. Both print and ebook formats are available online.

Find more titles and sign up to our readers' newsletter at www.collectiveinkbooks.com/business-books